W9-DFW-251

DISCARD

Ligonier Elementary
Media Center
610 Grand Street
Ligonier, IN 46767

Issue #1
Spring 2004

biography for beginners

Sketches for Early Readers

Laurie Lanzen Harris,
Editor

Favorable Impressions

P.O. Box 69018
Pleasant Ridge, Michigan 48069

Laurie Lanzen Harris, *Editor and Publisher*
Dan Harris, *Vice President, Marketing*
Favorable Impressions
P.O. Box 69018, Pleasant Ridge, Michigan 48069

Copyright © 2004 Laurie Lanzen Harris

ISSN 1081-4973

All rights reserved. No part of this publication may be reproduced or transmitted in any form or by any means, electronic or mechanical, including photocopy, recording, or any information storage and retrieval system, without permission in writing from the publisher.

The information in this publication was compiled from the sources cited and from other sources considered reliable. While every possible effort has been made to ensure reliability, the publisher will not assume liability for damages caused by inaccuracies in the data, and makes no warranty, express or implied, on the accuracy of the information contained herein.

∞

This book is printed on acid-free paper meeting the ANSI Z39.48 Standard. The infinity symbol that appears above indicates that the paper in this book meets that standard.

Printed in the United States

Contents

Preface

Biography for Beginners is a publication designed for young readers ages 6 to 9. It covers the kinds of people young people want to know about—favorite authors, television and sports stars, and world figures.

Biography for Beginners is published two times a year. A one-year subscription includes two 100-page hardbound volumes, published in Spring (May) and Fall (October).

The Plan of the Work

Biography for Beginners is especially created for young readers in a format they can read, understand, and enjoy. Each hardcover issue contains approximately 10 profiles, arranged alphabetically. Each entry provides several illustrations, including photographs of the individual, book covers, illustrations from books, and action shots. Each entry is coded with a symbol that indicates the profession of the person profiled. Boldfaced headings lead readers to information on birth, growing up, school, choosing a career, work life, and home and family. Each entry concludes with an address so that students can write for further information. Web sites are included as available. The length and vocabulary used in each entry, as well as the type size, page size, illustrations, and layout, have been developed with early readers in mind.

Because an early reader's first introduction to biography often comes as part of a unit on a writer like Dr. Seuss, authors are a special focus of *Biography for Beginners*. The authors included in this issue were chosen for their appeal to readers in grades one through four.

There is a broad range of reading abilities in children ages 6 to 9. A book that would appeal to a beginning first-grade reader might not satisfy the needs of an advanced reader finishing the fourth grade. To accommodate the widest range of readers in the age group, *Biography for Beginners* is written at the mid-second grade to third grade reading level. If beginning readers find the content too difficult, the entry could be used as a "read aloud" text, or readers could use the boldfaced headings to focus on parts of a sketch.

Indexes

Each issue of *Biography for Beginners* includes a Name Index, a Subject Index covering occupations and ethnic and minority backgrounds, and a Birthday Index. These indexes cumulate with each issue. The indexes are intended to be used by the young readers themselves, with help from teachers and librarians, and are not as detailed or lengthy as the indexes in works for older children.

Our Advisors

Biography for Beginners was reviewed by an Advisory Board made up of school librarians, public librarians, and reading specialists. Their thoughtful comments and suggestions have been invaluable in developing this publication. Any errors, however, are mine alone. I would like to list the members of the Advisory Board and to thank them again for their efforts.

Gail Beaver   University of Michigan School of Information
                    Ann Arbor, MI

Nancy Bryant   Brookside School Library
                    Cranbrook Educational Community
                    Bloomfield Hills, MI

Linda Carpino   Detroit Public Library
                    Detroit, MI

Helen Gregory   Grosse Pointe Public Library
                    Grosse Pointe, MI

Your Comments Are Welcome

Our goal is to provide accurate, accessible biographical information to early readers. Let us know how you think we're doing. Please write or call me with your comments.

We want to include the people your young readers want to know about. Send me your suggestions to the address below, or to my e-mail address. You can also post suggestions at our website, www.favimp.com. If we include someone you or a young reader suggest, we will send you a free issue, with our compliments, and we'll list your name in the issue in which your suggested profile appears.

And take a look at the next page, where we've listed those libraries and individuals who will be receiving a free copy of this issue for their suggestions.

Acknowledgments

I'd like to thank Mary Ann Stavros for superb design, layout, and typesetting; Cherie Abbey for editorial assistance; Barry Puckett for research assistance; and Kevin Hayes for production help.

Laurie Harris
Editor, *Biography for Beginners*
P.O. Box 69018
Pleasant Ridge, MI 48069
e-mail: Llanzenh@aol.com
URL: http://www.favimp.com

CONGRATULATIONS!

Congratulations to the following individuals and libraries, who are receiving a free copy of *Biography for Beginners*, Spring 2004, for suggesting people who appear in this issue:

Sister Jeanette Adler, Pine Ridge Elementary School, Birdseye, IN
Carol Blaney, Conley Elementary School, Whitman, MA
Karen Locke, McKean Elementary School, McKean, PA
Carolyn Malden, Manito School, Oakland, NJ

Tiki (left) and Ronde (right) Barber.

Ronde and Tiki Barber
1975-
American Professional Football Players

RONDE AND TIKI BARBER WERE BORN on April 7, 1975, in Montgomery County, Virginia. They are identical twins, and Ronde is seven minutes older than Tiki. Their parents are Geraldine and James Barber. When they were little, Geraldine worked for the Girl Scouts. James was a college football star and later played in the world football league.

"Ronde" and "Tiki" are their nicknames. An African friend of the family helped name them. Ronde's full name is Jamael Orondo, which means "first-born son." Tiki's is Atiim Kiambu, which means "fiery-tempered king."

They've always looked just alike. When they were little only their mom could tell them apart. She had to write their names on the bottom of their shoes so the babysitter could tell who was who.

RONDE AND TIKI BARBER GREW UP in Roanoke, Virginia. Their parents divorced when they were four. They were raised by their mom and never had much contact with their father.

Ronde and Tiki have always been very close to their mother. As a single parent, she worked hard to provide for them. When they were growing up, she worked all day for the Girl Scouts. At night, after they went to bed, she did work at home for an insurance company. It was important to her that her boys live in a good neighborhood and go to good schools.

Geraldine Barber taught her kids about money when they were very young. "I can remember when the kids wanted stuff they couldn't afford," she says. "I would say, 'Here is my paycheck. Here are the things I have to pay for: rent, car insurance. Whatever is left, you can have.' They saw early that you can't get your paycheck and just go out and have fun."

RONDE AND TIKI BAR-BER WENT TO SCHOOL at the Roanoke public schools. They were both excellent students, and they were great athletes, too. One of their coaches from elementary school still remembers them. "They could fly," he says.

Ronde runs for a touchdown after making an interception.

Ronde and Tiki were very competitive, but they always chose differ-ent positions in sports. In football, Ronde always played defense. Tiki played offense. They both went out for track, but chose separate events. Ronde ran the hurdles, and Tiki did the long jump. In baseball, Ronde played centerfield and Tiki pitched.

But they could be competitive when it was just the two of them. "If you put us in the backyard together for a whiffle-ball game or a flag football match, well, that could get pretty ugly, and downright competitive," remembers Ronde.

Tiki Barber breaks away from a tackler and heads for the end zone.

Still, says their mom, they were as close as could be. "I think growing up they knew that regardless of how bad things got, they thought, 'I always have my brother.' They could say: 'I will never be in this world by myself'."

SCHOOL, SPORTS, AND SUPPORT FROM MOM: Geraldine Barber was very strict. The boys were great athletes even as kids, but she made it clear that school always came first. They had to finish their homework everyday before practice. She was also a great supporter of their teams. She's rarely missed a game since the boys were in high school.

Ronde and Tiki went to Cave Spring High School in Roanoke, Virginia. They shone in the classroom, and in sports, too. As seniors, they shared the Athlete of the Year award. In track, they set state records. They graduated with honors, and Tiki was the top student in the class.

There are many funny stories about the twins switching places. As a senior, Tiki was voted the school "Knight," for outstanding academics and athletics. He was supposed to march in a parade before the final football game. His coach didn't like that. Finally, the principal came up with the perfect solution. Ronde was injured and wasn't playing in the game, so he marched in Tiki's place, and no one ever knew the difference.

COLLEGE: Ronde and Tiki both decided to go to college at the University of Virginia. There, they continued their winning ways on and off the field. They both played football, won awards, and set records. They roomed together, and they both majored in business. They did so well in school and football that they were both Academic All-Americans. They graduated in 1997 and prepared for their biggest challenge—pro football.

PLAYING PRO FOOTBALL: In 1997, Ronde and Tiki entered the "draft" for the National Football League (NFL). In the draft, teams pick athletes to play for them. Ronde was chosen by the Tampa Bay Buccaneers. Tiki was picked by the New York Giants. For the first time in their lives, the brothers had to live apart.

It was hard. "I always had somebody," recalled Tiki. "Then suddenly you get separated from someone you have seen every day for 21 years. I think up to that point,

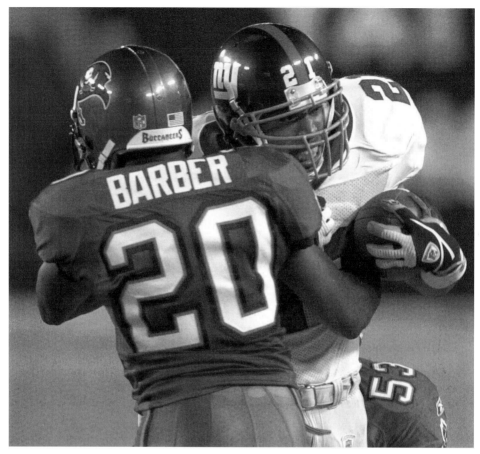

Ronde (20) takes down his brother Tiki (21) during a game that was broadcast on "Monday Night Football," November 24, 2003.

we had been apart for maybe a day. Those first months without each other, it made for some big phone bills."

TIKI AND THE NEW YORK GIANTS: Since 1997, Tiki Barber has been one of the best players on the New York Giants. He is a running back, a position on the offense. That means he takes the ball and runs with it, and also catches passes. In his rookie season, he ran for over 900 yards and four touchdowns. The next year, 1998, he totaled more than 500 yards and three touchdowns.

The 1999 season was a great one for Tiki. He put together 1,639 total yards. That included a Giants' record of 231 yards in just one game. The 2000 season was even better. Tiki played in every game, and became the first Giant ever to reach 2,000 yards in one season. In 2001, Tiki played in 14 games, but was injured. Even so, he led the team in total yards, and helped his team reach the Super Bowl.

Tiki's 2002 season was his best so far. He played in all 16 games. He led the Giants and the NFC conference with 1,984 total yards. In 2003 he continued his winning ways. By the end of the season, Tiki had 9,069 total yards, the second-best record in the team's history.

RONDE AND THE TAMPA BAY BUCCANEERS: In 1997, Ronde started to play with the Tampa Bay Buccaneers. As a "cornerback" on the defense, Ronde's job is to tackle receivers, intercept the football, and sack quarterbacks. He does it all extremely well. He's one of the finest defensive backs in the NFL.

In 1997, Ronde played in just two games. But in 1998, he showed what he could do. He played in 16 games and led all the cornerbacks in tackles and defended passes. The 1999 season was another great one, with Ronde playing in all the Buc's games and making 74 tackles.

In 2000, Ronde once again played in all the regular games and one playoff. He was named NFC Player of the Week early in the season. He also led all other players in sacks. In 2001 Ronde was in great form. He made the Pro Bowl and was named to All-NFL and All-Pro teams. He made NFL Defensive Back of the Year, too. His 10 interceptions and total defended passes ranked him first on his team.

The 2002 Buccaneers went all the way to the Super Bowl, with Ronde leading the way. Despite injuries, he played in all the regular and playoff games. The Bucs' defensive unit was the best in the NFL, and Ronde played his part. He had 95 tackles, three sacks, and defended against 21 passes. And when the Bucs won the big game, Ronde got his Super Bowl ring. The 2003 season didn't find the Bucs in the Super Bowl again, but it was still a great one for Ronde. And it featured a match up that pitted the twins against each other.

Playing Against Each Other: The brothers have played against each other several times in their careers. In the fall of 2003, they faced each other in a game on "Monday Night Football." Because they're such popular players, the game got a lot of coverage. Their mom wasn't sure if she could watch. "There are two things I do before every game," she said. "I call their cellphones and remind them to play proud. And I say a silent prayer they are able to walk off that field." The Bucs defeated the Giants in a terrific game.

Ronde (left) with his mom and Tiki after the Bucs won the Super Bowl, January 2003.

Even with their demanding jobs, the brothers have managed to stay close. They talk to each other almost every day. And even though they're competitive, they're also each other's biggest supporter. "The funny thing is that we've never been competitive in a negative way," says Ronde. "I'm his biggest fan and he's my biggest fan. I'm his biggest critic and he's my biggest critic. We want to see each other do well. I've never wanted to beat him in front of other people. No way do I ever want to see him fail."

"Tiki is the best running back in the NFL," says Ronde. "Ronde is the best cornerback in the National

Tiki reads to kids attending the Barbers'
summer football camp.

Football League," says Tiki. "We believe in each other and motivate each other. That's a big part of why we're so successful."

TIKI BARBER'S HOME AND FAMILY: Tiki married his college sweetheart, Ginny Cha, in 1999. They have one son, A.J., and are expecting another baby. They live in New York City in a large apartment.

Tiki loves to wear nice clothes, and he has his own radio and television show. After his playing days are over, he'd love to be a football commentator on TV. His favorite books are the *Harry Potter* series.

QUOTE

Tiki said this about being a twin.

"There is a bond there that people don't understand. We're, in essence, the same person. It's never going to end. It's never going to be a situation where you feel like this person is distrustful of you. I know I am always going to get honest opinions. I know I am always going to have someone who is telling me things I need to hear and not what I want to hear. And that's why it's so special."

RONDE BARBER'S HOME AND FAMILY: Ronde's wife is named Claudia. They have two girls, Yammile and Justyce. He's also active in many charities, especially for kids. The twins have appeared on posters encouraging kids to read.

The brothers still spend time together whenever they can. Every summer, they go back to Roanoke and run a football camp for the local kids. And they're working on a children's book called *By My Brother's Side*.

Ronde and Tiki are still very close to their mom. In 2003, when she turned 50, they bought her a new house and a fancy new Corvette. They are very proud of all she's done. "She is our mentor," says Tiki. "When we went off to college, she went back and got her M.B.A. with straight A's."

FOR MORE INFORMATION ABOUT RONDE BARBER:

Write: The Tampa Bay Buccaneers
Raymond James Stadium
One Buccaneers Place
Tampa, FL 33607

WORLD WIDE WEB SITE:

http://www.buccaneers.com/team/playerdetail.aspx/
  player=Barber,Ronde

FOR MORE INFORMATION ABOUT TIKI BARBER:

Write: The New York Giants
Giants Stadium
East Rutherford, NJ 07073

WORLD WIDE WEB SITE:

http://www.giants.com/team/playerpage.cfm?
  player_id=5719

Ludwig Bemelmans
1898-1962
Austrian-Born American Author and Illustrator
Creator of *Madeline*

LUDWIG BEMELMANS WAS BORN on April 27, 1898, in Meran, Austria. Meran is in the mountains, in an area known as the Tyrol. When Bemelmans was growing up, the area was part of Austria. Now, it is part of Italy. His parents were Lambert and Frances Bemelmans. Lambert was a painter and Frances was a homemaker.

LUDWIG BEMELMANS GREW UP in a small town in Austria, where his family lived in a hotel. He spent his first six years there. He remembered that he met other guests, like "Russian grand dukes and English lords." Ludwig much preferred being with the servants. He didn't have many friends his own age, and he was often lonely. Sometimes he would slip away from the hotel to find children to play with.

When Ludwig was eight, his parents divorced. He and his mother went to live with her family in Regensburg, Germany.

LUDWIG BEMELMANS WENT TO SCHOOL at many different schools. He was a rebel, and he got into a lot of trouble. By the age of 14, he'd been kicked out of several schools. His mother decided he should try working.

FIRST JOBS: Bemelmans got a job with an uncle who owned hotels. Over the next few years, Bemelmans worked in several hotels, but his hot temper got the best of him. He was fired from several jobs, and his mother didn't know what to do. She told him he could either go to reform school, or to America.

COMING TO AMERICA: On Christmas Eve in 1914, at the age of 16, Ludwig Bemelmans arrived in America. He traveled alone, on a boat that landed in New York City.

All he had with him were letters introducing him to hotel owners in New York.

Over the next several years Bemelmans worked in many different hotels. But his unusual ways often lost him jobs. Once, he was fired for wearing one white shoe and one yellow shoe to work. In 1917, Bemelmans got a job as a waiter at the Ritz-Carlton. That's one of the fanciest hotels in New York. But when the U.S. entered World War I that year, Bemelmans left his job to join the Army. He used his German-language skills to help other German immigrants train to be soldiers. He also worked for a time in an army hospital.

After the war ended in 1918, Bemelmans went back to work at the Ritz. He also became an American citizen. During this time, he began to study art. He loved to paint and draw. He took classes whenever he could afford it.

In 1925, after years of working for others, Bemelmans started his own business. He opened a restaurant, called the Hapsburg House.

The Hapsburg House combined all the things Bemelmans loved: cooking and serving customers, and art, too. He painted murals on the walls. In his apartment, he painted scenes on the window shades. The apartment walls were full of drawings of fancy furniture. He couldn't

afford real tables and chairs, but his "art" furniture was beautiful.

One of Bemelmans's neighbors saw his work and thought it was wonderful. He knew a woman who worked for a children's book publisher. Her name was May Massee. The neighbor introduced Massee to Bemelmans.

STARTING TO WRITE FOR CHILDREN: Massee thought Bemelmans was an amazing artist. She encouraged him to write and illustrate a book for children. Massee worked for Viking Press, and they published Bemelmans's first book, *Hansi*, in 1934. Like all his books, it is based, in part, on his own past. *Hansi* tells the story of two children growing up among the Austrian mountains. Its lovely watercolor illustrations help tell this tale of his childhood home.

MADELINE: In 1939, Bemelmans published the book that made him one of the best-loved children's authors of all time. "In an old house in Paris that was covered with vines," it begins. It is, of course, *Madeline*, a favorite with readers all over the world.

Children, and adults, too, love the story of the feisty Madeline and her school friends. Readers delight in the story of the girls and their daily lives with their teacher, Miss Clavell. The story is told in rhyme, as the girls, "in two straight lines," went for walks, "broke their bread, and brushed their teeth, and went to bed." Then, calamity strikes. Madeline must go to the hospital and have her appendix out! But everything turns out just

fine. Madeline faces it all with great bravery, and afterwards, she even has a *scar*.

Readers young and old love the story of Madeline. Bemelmans tells the tale with great wit and warmth. The illustrations, too, are lively and beautiful. He used vivid watercolors to paint many scenes of Paris, from gardens to churches.

Madeline returned again in *Madeline's Rescue*. In this story, Madeline falls into a river and is rescued by a stray dog. All ends well, as the dog is adopted by Madeline and her friends. *Madeline's Rescue* won the Caldecott Medal in 1953. That's the highest honor in children's book illustration.

Bemelmans wrote four more books featuring the lively Madeline. They include *Madeline and the Bad Hat, Madeline and the Gypsies,* and *Madeline in London.* His last book, *Madeline's Christmas*, was published in 1985, after his death. The books have also been made into popular movies. They've been translated into many languages. The little Paris schoolgirl has become one of the most beloved characters in the world.

Bemelmans named his famous character for his wife, Madeleine. He based the character on his mother's memories of growing up, and also on his own daughter, Barbara.

OTHER BOOKS FOR CHILDREN: In addition to his *Madeline* tales, Bemelmans wrote several other books for children. One, *Parsley,* tells the story of a stag that lives in the forest near the Tyrolean mountains. Another, *Quito Express*, is about the adventures of a little boy in Ecuador.

BOOKS AND ART FOR ADULTS: Bemelmans wrote many books for adults, too. He loved to travel, and some of his books are based on his journeys. He also wrote about his life and his experiences running a restaurant. Bemelmans continued to paint, and his illustrations appeared in magazines like *The New Yorker*. One of his most famous paintings is in the Carlyle Hotel in New York City.

LUDWIG BEMELMANS'S HOME AND FAMILY: Bemelmans married Madeleine Freund in 1935. They had one daughter, Barbara. He lived and worked in New York City. In his later years he wrote, painted, and traveled. Ludwig Bemelmans died of cancer on October 1, 1962, at the age of 64.

QUOTE

"Does one ever see things clearer
than as a child?"

SOME OF LUDWIG BEMELMANS'S BOOKS:

The *Madeline* Books

Madeline

Madeline's Rescue

Madeline and the Bad Hat

Madeline and the Gypsies

Madeline in London

Madeline's Christmas

Other Books for Young Readers

Hansi

The Golden Basket

The Castle Number Nine

Quito Express

Fifi

Rosebud

Sunshine: A Story about the City of New York

The Happy Place

The High World

Parsley

FOR MORE INFORMATION ABOUT LUDWIG BEMELMANS:

Write: Viking Penguin
375 Hudson St.
New York, NY 10014

WORLD WIDE WEB SITES:

http://www.arlingtoncemetary.net/lbemelmans.htm
http://www.kidsreads.com/series/series-madeline-author.
asp

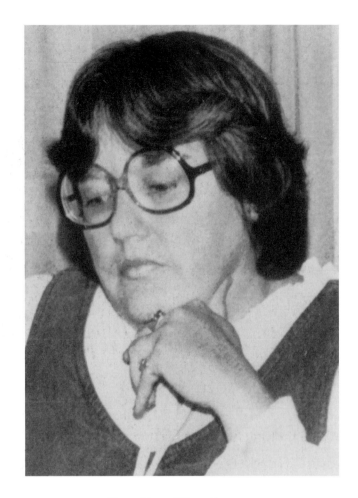

Judy Delton

1931-2001
American Author of Books for Children
Creator of the "Pee Wee Scouts" Books

JUDY DELTON WAS BORN on May 6, 1931, in St. Paul, Minnesota. Delton became her last name when she married. Her last name growing up was Jaschke. Her parents were A.F. and Alice Jaschke. Her father was an engineer and her mother was a homemaker.

JUDY DELTON GREW UP in St. Paul. Her family was Catholic, and she grew up in an area where most of her neighbors were Catholic, too. The memories of that time stayed with her. Years later, she recreated her early life in her "Kitty" series.

JUDY DELTON WENT TO SCHOOL at the Catholic schools in St. Paul. She went to art school after high school, and then studied for a teaching degree. In 1957, she graduated from the College of St. Catherine and started to teach.

FIRST JOBS: Delton was a teacher in the Catholic schools in St. Paul for several years. She taught elementary school, and she loved it. She got married in 1958, and soon she had children. She decided to leave teaching in 1964. She wanted to do something that would allow her to stay home with her kids.

STARTING TO WRITE FOR CHILDREN: Delton began to write poetry and essays for magazines. Then she started to write for children. Over the next 30 years, she wrote over 100 books. Many of these appeared in series, including the "Kitty" books, the "Angel" books, and "The Pee Wee Scouts."

Delton's first book was *Two Good Friends*. It was published in 1974, and it was a success. From that point

on, Delton wrote most of her books for young readers. She loved writing for kids. She said she "branched out into children's books, where I've stayed comfortable ever since."

"KITTY": Delton's first popular books were those about a character named Kitty. The books were based on her own memories of growing up in the 1940s. They focus on Kitty's life as she faces new challenges, like moving and going to a new school. The books relate her experiences in a warm, understanding way.

"THE PEE WEE SCOUTS": Delton's most popular series by far is "The Pee Wee Scouts." The first book in the series was *Cookies and Crutches.* Since then, more than 40 books have appeared in the series, and they've sold millions of copies. The books feature the adventures of a group of elementary school kids.

The Pee Wee Scouts earn their badges in all sorts of ways. From reading books to collecting trash, from

camping to decorating for the holidays, the girls have hilarious adventures. Kids love the characters, especially Molly, and the scout leader, Mrs. Peters.

Illustrated by Jill Weber

ANGEL: Another series that is popular with young readers features a character named Angel. She's always worrying about something, and Delton tells her stories with warmth and humor. In *Angel Spreads Her Wings*, she travels to Greece, anxious about everything from a new stepdad's family to having to eat fish with the head on. In *Angel Bites the Bullet*, she has to share her room when a family friend moves in.

Delton based Angel on the experiences of her daughter Jennifer. Angel appeared in five books altogether. They have become a popular series with many grade school readers.

WHERE DID SHE GET HER IDEAS? Delton always said that her own life was the source of her ideas. "Someone once said that an author is fortunate in that he gets to live his life twice, once in the doing and once in the telling. I find that to be true, since I am always reliving my life." Still, she said, it was the *feelings* of what it was like to be a child that she tried to recapture. "What I use from my own life is not the facts, it's the emotion. It's how I felt about something. It has nothing to do with facts at all. You can get those anywhere. It's the feelings of childhood that you need to know."

In addition to her many children's books, Delton also wrote articles for magazines. She helped other writers become children's authors, too. She wrote a book to help them called *The 29 Most Common Writing Mistakes and How to Avoid Them*. She also held writing workshops in her home, and she created a newspaper column about writing for children.

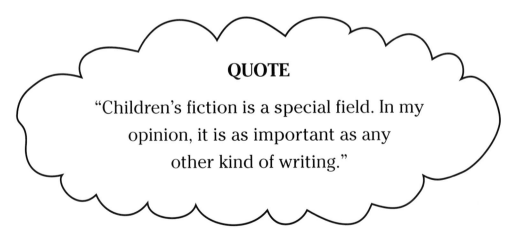

QUOTE

"Children's fiction is a special field. In my opinion, it is as important as any other kind of writing."

JUDY DELTON'S HOME AND FAMILY: Delton married her husband, Jeff, in 1958. They had four children, Julie, Jina, Jennifer, and Jamie. Her family was very important to her life and work. She left teaching to stay at home with them, and she also featured two of her children, Jennifer and Jamie, in her books. Judy Delton died in St. Paul on December 31, 2001, at the age of 70.

SOME OF JUDY DELTON'S BOOKS:

"Pee Wee Scouts" Series

Cookies and Crutches
Camp Ghost-Away
Lucky Dog Days
Blue Skies, French Fries
Grumpy Pumpkins
Peanut-Butter Pilgrims
A Pee Wee Christmas
That Mushy Stuff
The Pooped Troop
The Pee Wee Jubilee
Bad, Bad Bunnies
Rosy Noses, Freezing Toes
Sonny's Secret
Sky Babies
Trash Bash
Pee Wees on Parade
Lights, Action, Land-Ho!
Piles of Pets
Fishy Wishes
Pee Wees on Skis

Greedy Groundhogs
All Dads on Deck
Tricks and Treats
Pee Wees on First
Super Duper Pee Wee
Teeny Weeny Zucchinis
Eggs with Legs
Pee Wee Pool Party
Bookworm Buddies
Molly for Mayor

"Angel" Series

Angel's Mother's Boyfriend
Angel's Mother's Baby
Angel in Charge
Angel Spreads Her Wings
Angel Bites the Bullet

"Kitty" Series

Kitty from the Start
Kitty in the Middle
Kitty in the Summer
Kitty in High School

Other Books:

Two Good Friends
Rabbit Finds a Way

Two Is Company
Brimhall Comes to Stay
Brimhall Turns to Magic
The Best Mom in the World

FOR MORE INFORMATION ABOUT JUDY DELTON:

Write: Bantam Doubleday Dell
1540 Broadway
New York, NY 10036

WORLD WIDE WEB SITE:

http://www.houghtonmifflinbooks.com

Raven

1985-
American Actress and Singer
Star of "That's So Raven" and *The Cheetah Girls*

RAVEN WAS BORN on December 10, 1985, in Atlanta, Georgia. Her full name is Raven-Symone Christina Pearman, but now she's known as Raven. Her parents are Lydia and Christopher Pearman. They both manage

Raven's career, and her dad also writes and produces music. She has a younger brother named Blaize.

Raven was named for an animal in the legend of Noah's Ark. After the flood, "Noah released the raven first," says her dad. "The raven is very, very intelligent. And to us, she was this beautiful black bird."

STARTING IN SHOW BUSINESS: Raven started in show business as a model. When she was 16 months old, she modeled for an Atlanta department store. Then she went on to print and television ads. She did TV commercials for Cheerios and Ritz Crackers before the age of three.

"THE COSBY SHOW": Raven loved "The Cosby Show" on television. The show is still on TV in reruns and still very popular. It starred Bill Cosby as Dr. Cliff Huxtable, and several young stars as his children. The youngest actress on the show was Keshia Knight Pullman, who played Rudy.

According to her parents, when Raven was two she said, "I can do what Rudy can do." She wanted to act, and she wanted to be on "The Cosby Show." So her parents took her to New York City, where the show was filmed. There, she tried out for a TV movie called *Ghost Dad*. She didn't get the part, but the producers loved her. They thought Bill Cosby would, too.

Phylicia Rashad, as Claire Huxtable, talks on the telephone while Bill Cosby, as Dr. Huxtable and other cast members of the family sitcom "The Cosby Show" gather around during taping of the final episode, March 6, 1992. Raven, as Olivia, is the fourth actor from the left.

Raven tried out for Bill Cosby, and he thought she was terrific. Soon, she became part of the show. She played Olivia, the stepdaughter of Lisa Bonet's character, Denise. She was on the show for three years, from 1989 to 1992.

Raven was a favorite with audiences and with Cosby, too. He said, "She is professional in every way. Raven comes to the studio on time, knows her lines, and is ready to work." Raven's dad helped her learn her lines by reading the scripts to her as if they were stories.

After "The Cosby Show" ended in 1992, Raven did some parts in other TV shows. She appeared in the TV movie *Queen*. She also had roles on "Sesame Street," "A Different World," and "The Fresh Prince of Bel-Air."

"HANGIN' WITH MR. COOPER": It wasn't long before Raven was working on another TV show. In 1993, she became part of the cast of "Hangin' with Mr. Cooper." The show starred Mark Curry, and Raven played his niece, Nicole. She loved it. "It's great working with Mark," she said. "He's real, real tall and real, real funny." Viewers loved Raven as Nicole. She played the part for four years.

RECORD ALBUMS: Raven always loved singing, and her parents arranged for her to make her first record in 1990. That first record was called *Here's to New Dreams*, and it came out in 1993. Her dad wrote several of the songs and helped produce the record, too.

Raven made another record in 1999, called *Undeniable*. It featured songs written by the R&B star Stevie Wonder. Raven got to work with him in the studio. "It was wonderful," she says. Raven wrote one of the songs on the record, called "Best Friend." To promote the album, Raven went on tour with the band N'SYNC.

MOVIES: The busy Raven also did movies while making TV shows and records. In 1994, she appeared in *The Little Rascals*. In 1999, she starred with the hilarious Eddie

Raven and Eddie Murphy in a scene from Dr. Doolittle 2.

Murphy in *Dr. Doolittle*. She played the part of Murphy's daughter Charisse. She remembers how Murphy tried to make his co-stars laugh during filming. "When the camera's rolling and the scene is supposed to be over, he keeps on going, and it's really hard to keep a straight face."

Raven appeared in the sequel, *Dr. Doolittle 2*, in 2001. She remembers all the animals she shared scenes with. Some, like the monkey Crystal, were great. "Crystal's really sweet, very friendly, and doesn't bite," she said. But others weren't so nice. "Once when I was holding the chameleon, he wouldn't let go of my hand. I was wearing lace and he kept sticking to it. They had to pull him off!"

In 1999, Raven appeared in the Disney TV movie *Zenon: Girl of the 21st Century*. She played the part of

Zenon's friend Nebula. That led to a role on the Disney Channel cartoon "Kim Possible." She started on the show in 2002, and still provides the voice of Monique.

"THAT'S SO RAVEN": Raven is best known to fans today as the star of "That's So Raven." She started on the show in 2003, and it's become a hit with kids. She plays Raven

The cast of "That's So Raven."

Raven, second from left, in The Cheetah Girls.

Baxter, a girl with special gifts. Raven can see into the future. But she really doesn't see exactly what's going to happen. And that's where things get funny.

"It's all about a girl who has psychic visions," Raven says. "However, as the visions are always incomplete, she has to figure out exactly what they mean. This often lands her and her friends in hot water." The cast has a great time. Raven loves "dressing up in strange and weird costumes. It's a real blast."

THE CHEETAH GIRLS: In 2003, Raven appeared in the TV movie *The Cheetah Girls*. She played Galleria

Garibaldi, a fashion- and music-loving teenager. Galleria's trying to get her girl group to win the high school talent show. Raven loved the opportunity to "act, sing, and dance," she said.

RAVEN WENT TO SCHOOL on the set of her TV shows and to a regular public school, too. When she was working on TV, she had a tutor for three hours a day. During some of her high school years, she attended North Springs High School in Atlanta. She loved being just a kid, and "having sleepovers and going shopping." That ended with the start of "That's So Raven." She finished up her high school courses with a tutor. Raven graduated from North Springs in the fall of 2003.

Raven would like to go to college, probably in California. But she doesn't plan on studying acting. "Hopefully, I will stay in the business," she says. "But it's very flaky and you never know if you're going to get a job. So when I get to college, what I major in is going to be something different than acting, just in case it doesn't work out."

Raven loves to cook. She thinks she might study cooking someday, too. And she might even start her own restaurant.

OTHER PROJECTS: Raven is still working on "That's So Raven" and "Kim Possible." In 2004, she'll start work

"Kim Possible."

on two movies, *All-American Girl* and *Sparkle*. She's keeping her hand in music, too. She's doing a soundtrack for "That's So Raven" and working on a new album.

RAVEN'S HOME AND FAMILY: Raven and her family have two homes, one in Atlanta and one in California. They spend part of the year in each. Raven is very close to her family.

In her spare time, Raven likes to hang out with friends and shop. She's also very active in charities. She's raised money for the March of Dimes, Juvenile Diabetes, and Ronald McDonald Houses. She also helps out with Disney's Adventure All-Star volunteer program.

QUOTE

Raven says that Bill Cosby gave her advice when she was five that she still remembers.

"'Stay professional and stay sweet', he told me. I haven't been the kid on the set that throws tantrums, even today. That advice still works. Thanks, Mr. Cosby."

SOME OF RAVEN'S CREDITS:

Television

"The Cosby Show"
"Hangin' with Mr. Cooper"
"Kim Possible"
"That's So Raven"
The Cheetah Girls

Movies

Dr. Doolittle
Dr. Doolittle 2

Recordings

Here's to New Dreams
Undeniable

FOR MORE INFORMATION ON RAVEN:

Write: Disney Channel
3800 West Almeda Ave.
Burbank, CA 91505

WORLD WIDE WEB SITE:

http://psc.disney.go.com/disneychannel/thatssoraven/

Eric Rohmann
1957-
American Artist and Author and
Illustrator of Children's Books
Creator of *My Friend Rabbit*

ERIC ROHMANN WAS BORN on October 26, 1957, in Riverside, Illinois. His parents are Harry and Phyllis Rohmann.

ERIC ROHMANN GREW UP in Downers Grove, a suburb of Chicago. He loved to play sports, especially baseball and hockey. He also loved to explore. He collected rocks, leaves, insects, and animal skulls.

"I spent my weekends and afternoons after school in the forests and fields just beyond the creek that ran in front of our house," he recalled. "I'd imagine I was in wild places or on some far-flung planet. I could never pass a fallen log without turning it over to see what lived underneath."

"In an effort to understand the things I'd discovered, I began to draw," he says. "The pictures I made took place in imaginary worlds by way of the fields and forests across from the creek."

ERIC ROHMANN WENT TO SCHOOL at the local public schools. He says he wasn't much of a reader, but remembers loving *The Snowy Day* by Ezra Jack Keats. He also loved the books of Dr. Seuss and Maurice Sendak.

"Sometime around fourth grade, I began to read anything that used pictures and words to tell stories," he recalls. "The Sunday funnies, picture books, the illustrated instructions for a model battleship."

Eric read plenty of comic books, too. "I thrilled at all those colored panels and word balloons," he says. "And it wasn't just the drawings, it was also that, page by page, the story unfolded before me. Comics always awakened my imagination, drew me into the stories, and suggested

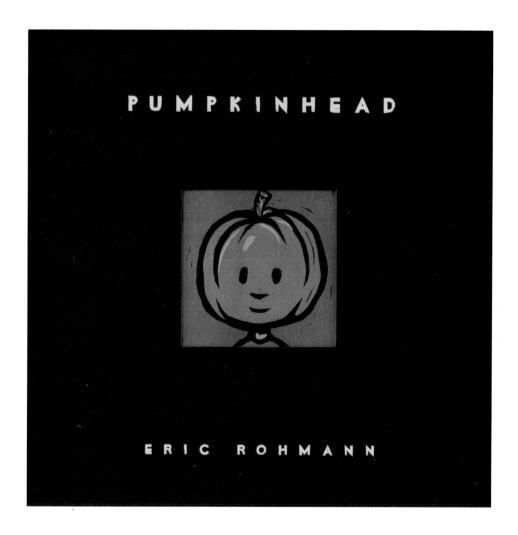

further adventures. I was right there with Tarzan or the Green Lantern." He started to create little comic books of his own. He called his first comic "Steve Star — Good Guy of the Galaxy."

Eric went to Downers Grove High School. He still loved nature, and he worked as a volunteer at the Brookfield Zoo in Chicago. He graduated from Downers Grove in 1975 and went on to college.

Rohmann went to Illinois State University, where he studied art. He got a bachelor's degree, then a master's degree at Illinois State. He continued his art studies at Arizona State University. At Arizona State, he also took courses in printmaking and fine bookmaking. These would help him later in his career as an author. After completing a master of fine arts degree at Arizona State, he began to teach.

FIRST JOBS: Rohmann taught painting, printmaking, and fine bookmaking at Belvoir Terrace in Boston, Massachusetts. Belvoir Terrace is a performing and visual arts program. He taught kids ages 7 to 17. "I started to see how their minds work," he says. "What they found funny, what they found fascinating. I discovered that a lot of that stuff I found fascinating and funny and interesting as well. So I decided to make books for them."

STARTING TO WRITE FOR CHILDREN: Rohmann's first book for kids, *Time Flies*, was turned down by 12 different publishers. Finally, Crown Publishing agreed to bring out the book. "When it sold, I was unemployed and pretty much at the end of my rope," he says. But the book was a success, and it launched his career in children's books.

TIME FLIES: *Time Flies* is a wordless picture book. Through his dreamy paintings, Rohmann tells the story of a bird flying through a natural history museum. As the bird flies into a room full of dinosaur skeletons, the scene comes to life. Suddenly, we are in the prehistoric world of real dinosaurs. One swallows the bird, but as the bird travels down his throat, time changes. The scene returns to the present. The dinosaur changes from flesh to bone, from life to skeleton. The bird flies away.

Children loved *Time Flies*. It won a Caldecott Honor award. That's an important honor for children's book illustration.

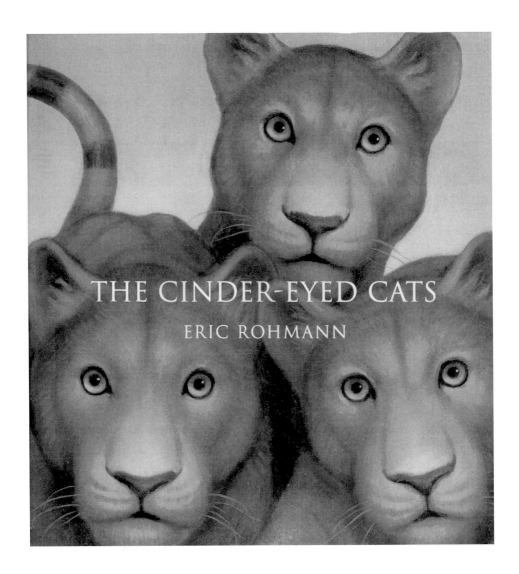

THE CINDER-EYED CATS: Rohmann's next book was *The Cinder-Eyed Cats*. It features a fantasy island full of beautiful, mysterious cats. Rohmann started out with sketches and rough paintings. For him, a book develops in the doing. He remembers that he "looked at lots of reference books, brochures of South Sea Islands, and visited the zoo whenever I was stuck."

Rohmann enjoys working with many different types of art media. "Oils and various printmaking techniques are the media I use most," he says. He usually starts out using "pencil, ink, watercolor, and oil washes. No surprise, these are also the media I know best."

MY FRIEND RABBIT: For his next book, Rohmann was ready for a change. First, he came up with an image. "It was a little animal doing something with a big animal — pushing it, pulling it, throwing it."

"*My Friend Rabbit* probably had a hundred words in it when I first started. I find that the more I make the pictures, the more they tell the story. What you try to do is have the words and the picture do different things. The words might describe smells or sounds, things that you don't know, or necessarily hear or see."

Next, he had to decide what art medium to use. "I started making pencil sketches, and then I realized that I wanted to use a different media. So I tried pastels. I tried watercolor. I tried pen and ink and scratch board. I made little paper sculptures."

Finally, he decided to use relief prints. He made them by using a linoleum-like material covered in ink. "I made one print and that seemed to make sense to me," he says. So he created a book with characters in bold black outlines. The result, *My Friend Rabbit*, has become a favorite with children everywhere.

My Friend Rabbit tells the story of two friends, Rabbit and Mouse. Rabbit plays with Mouse's airplane, and it gets stuck in a tree. Rabbit has an idea. He finds a strange assortment of animals and stacks them one on top of the other, to reach the plane. The stack of animals — a rhino, a hippo, an alligator, and more — topple to the ground. Soon, Rabbit and Mouse are on the run again, this time from the angry mob of animals.

THE CALDECOTT MEDAL: Kids love *My Friend Rabbit*, and adults do, too. The book won the Caldecott Medal in 2003. Rohmann couldn't believe it. He says that when he got the call telling him he'd won, he thought it was a joke.

It was 6am Chicago time, and he got up to answer the phone. He remembers that his arms and legs felt "like stale Twizzlers."

"The voice says, 'This is Pat Scales of the American Library Association'," he recalls. "My first thought is that I have overdue books." But instead, he'd won the most important award in children's book illustration. He was shocked. And amazed. He felt "surprised, overwhelmed, perplexed, astonished, exalted, joyful, and humbled," he said.

The award came just in time. Rohmann wasn't making much money from his children's books. In fact, he was just about to give up. "I had pretty much decided that if the new books didn't do well, I might start looking for something else to do. Now I feel I can keep doing books, and I don't have to go out and get a job!"

IS HE LIKE MOUSE, OR RABBIT? "I would say I'm mouse," says Rohmann. "In fact — not to give some great secret away — if you look at all my books up till now, the bird in *Time Flies*, the boy in *Cinder-Eyed Cats* — things happen to them. In some ways, they are all observers, and so is Mouse. I think I'm one of those people. I spend a lot of time looking at the world like Mouse. I've never known anybody like Rabbit, but I've always, in some ways, wanted to be that carefree. But I've never been able to do it."

NEW BOOKS:
Rohmann's most recent book is *Pumpkinhead.* He's working on another book about a girl named Clara and her imaginary friend—a huge fish!

ILLUSTRATING FOR OTHERS: Rohmann has illustrated the work of other authors, too. He created the jacket covers for Philip Pullman's well-known trilogy, *His Dark Materials.* Pullman loves the illustrations. He says that he was astonished when he saw the cover for the first book in the series, *The Golden Compass.* It features the character Lyra. Pullman said that Rohmann had painted her "as she truly is, better than I could ever have hoped to see her pictured."

ON WRITING FOR YOUNG READERS: Rohmann has great respect for his young readers. "I've found children are the best audience. They are enthusiastic, impulsive, generous, and pleased by simple joys. They laugh easily at the ridiculous and are willing to believe the absurd. They are hopeful, open-minded, and openhearted. To a child, every day is a great invention."

ERIC ROHMANN'S HOME AND FAMILY: Rohmann, who is single, works out of his home studio in La Grange, Illinois. He doesn't have kids of his own. One young reader was curious about that. "A little boy once wanted to know if I had kids," he recalls. "When I said no, he asked if I had any cats or pet mice or rabbits. When I said no, he said, 'You write books for kids about cats and mice and rabbits, but you don't have any. Are you sure you really write those books? I need proof'."

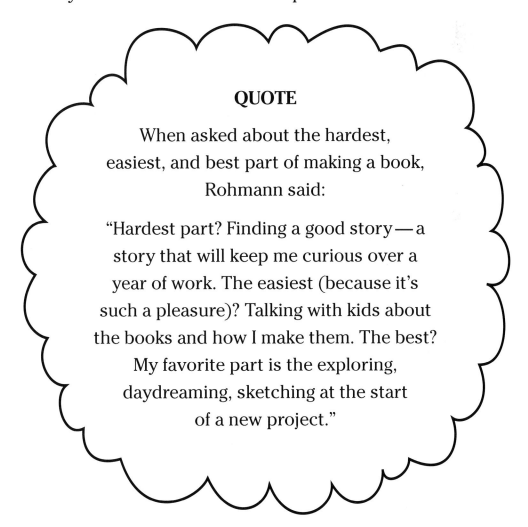

QUOTE

When asked about the hardest, easiest, and best part of making a book, Rohmann said:

"Hardest part? Finding a good story—a story that will keep me curious over a year of work. The easiest (because it's such a pleasure)? Talking with kids about the books and how I make them. The best? My favorite part is the exploring, daydreaming, sketching at the start of a new project."

SOME OF ERIC ROHMANN'S BOOKS

As Author and Illustrator

Time Flies
The Cinder-Eyed Cats
My Friend Rabbit
Pumpkinhead

As Illustrator

His Dark Materials: The Golden Compass, The Subtle Knife, The Amber Spyglass (by Philip Pullman)
King Crow (by Jennifer Armstrong)
The Prairie Train (by Antoine O. Flatharta)

FOR MORE INFORMATION ON ERIC ROHMANN:

Write: Roaring Brook Press
c/o The Millbrook Press
2 Old New Milford Rd.
Brookfield, CT 06804

WORLD WIDE WEB SITE:

http://www.scbwisocal.org.htmls/rohmann.htm

Michelle Wie

1989-
American Amateur Golfer
Youngest Player in History to Compete in
a PGA Tournament

MICHELLE WIE WAS BORN on October 11, 1989, in Honolulu, Hawaii. Her full name is Michelle Sung Wie, and her last name is pronounced "wee." Her parents are B.J. and Bo Wie. Her dad is a college professor and her mom is a homemaker. They are both from Korea.

MICHELLE WIE GREW UP in Hawaii. She still lives there now.

STARTING TO PLAY GOLF: When she was just four years old, Michelle started to play golf. Her dad was her teacher, and he was amazed at how well she could play.

THE GAME OF GOLF: In golf, the object is to take the least amount of shots, called "strokes," to get from the beginning of each hole to the end. A round of golf usually includes 18 holes. Each hole is supposed to be finished in a certain number of strokes. If a golfer completes the hole in that number, he or she has gotten a "par" for that hole. The player with the least amount of strokes wins the game.

From the time she was little, Michelle had an incredibly powerful swing. When she was seven, she played her first 18-hole round. She finished just 14 over par. By the time she was nine, she was beating her dad. She could also beat her mom, who was a former Korean golf champion.

Michelle could hit the ball with such force that by the time she was 10, she could shoot par. At that age, she became the youngest player ever to qualify for a USGA amateur tournament. (The USGA is the "United States Golf Association.") An "amateur" is someone who plays a sport as a nonprofessional. At some point, Wie will turn "pro" and play as a professional.

Wie drives from the tee at the Sony Open, January, 2004.

By the age of 11, Wie was winning most of the tournaments she entered. She won the Hawaii State Women's Stroke Play Championship in 2001. She was the youngest winner ever. She won the Jennie K. Wilson Invitational that year, too. Once again, she was the youngest winner in the tournament's history. She was hitting the ball farther than most men. Her dad, who was her caddie in those early years, thought she was ready for more challenges. She wanted to play with better players, and he encouraged her.

A STRING OF "FIRSTS": Soon, Wie was adding to her incredible string of "firsts."

In March 2002, Michelle played in her first LPGA tournament. The LPGA is the "Ladies Professional Golf Association." Just 12 years old, Wie was the youngest person ever to qualify for an LPGA event. People who saw her play just couldn't believe it. She was hitting the ball an incredible 280 yards on average. That's as far as many male pros hit the ball. She didn't make the final round, but she felt good about her game. "I'm not disappointed, I'm just happy to be here," she said. "There's free food and drinks and nobody bothers you on the practice greens."

Also in 2002, Wie played in the Woman's Amateur Public Links Championship. She made the semifinals, becoming the youngest person ever to do that.

By this point, Wie had grown to be six feet tall. Her body is strong, and she used that strength to improve her game.

There are three major challenges in golf. One is the "driving" part of the game, in which you try to hit the ball from the tee as far and as straight as you can. The second is called the "short game." In that part, you try to hit the ball from the fairway toward the hole. It is a shorter distance, and the challenge is to avoid the water and sand traps that often surround the hole. The third major challenge in golf is putting. Once the ball is on the part of the course called the "green," the golfer uses a club called a "putter" to place the ball in the hole.

Wie getting ready to put.

PLAYING WITH THE MEN: Michelle continued to work on her game, and she got better in every category. In January 2003, she decided to try playing against professional men golfers. She tried to qualify for the PGA Sony Open. The PGA is the "Professional Golf Association." Its members are all men. Wie was the only female competitor. She didn't make it, but she was determined to keep trying.

In February 2003, Wie was the only female in the Hawaii Pearl Open, a pro event. She did well, placing 43rd.

In March 2003, Wie played in her first major LPGA tournament, the Kraft Nabisco Championship. She played so well that she made the final round, paired with Annika Sorenstam. Sorenstam is one of the best women golfers.

She made headlines in 2003 as one of just three women to play with men in professional tournaments.

Wie finished ninth at the tournament and faced a mob of fans. "The attention was a little crazy, but I was really excited," she said. "I hope it shows how much practice pays off."

In June 2003, Wie entered the record books again. She became the youngest player ever to win the Women's Amateur Public Links.

That August, Wie played with the men again in the Canadian Tours' Bay Mills Open Championship. She missed the semifinals by just five strokes. In September 2003, she was the only female player in the Nationwide Tournament's Boise Open. She didn't make the semifinals, but she played well.

PLAYING IN A PGA TOUR EVENT: In January 2004, Wie broke another barrier. She played in her first PGA Tour event. Only three other women had played in a PGA Tour event before. And Michelle was the youngest person, ever, to play.

The event she played in was the Sony Open, held in Hawaii. Wie was trying to make the "cut." That means she was trying to shoot a low enough score to play in the championship round of the Open. On January 15, she shot just one stroke over the cutoff.

Wie hits out of a sandtrap.

Wie was disappointed. "Just one more shot, and I would have made it," she said. "It's killing me now." But pro golf watchers are sure that she'll just keep getting better and better.

Some of her biggest fans are the men on the PGA Tour who thought at first that she couldn't make it. "She probably has one of the best golf swings I've ever seen, period," said golf great Davis Love III. "Plus she's tall and strong. No telling what she's going to do when she gets a little older."

Another big fan is PGA great Tom Lehman. He nick-named Michelle "Big Wiesy" because her big, powerful

Wie with some of the greatest golfers of all time. From left to right, Arnold Palmer, Tom Watson, Wie, Lee Trevino, and Jack Nicklaus.

swing reminds him of Ernie Els. Els, who's called "Big Easy," is one of the best players in the game today.

Wie practices golf four hours a day during the week and seven hours on the weekends. It's one sport where you really need to put in the hours, and Wie does that. Her dad doesn't caddie for her anymore, but he still provides support and coaching for his amazing daughter.

MICHELLE WIE GOES TO SCHOOL at the Punahou School in Honolulu. She is an excellent student and gets mostly As. She missed a geometry test to play in the Sony tournament, but she always makes up her work immediately.

FUTURE PLANS: Wie's idol is PGA star Tiger Woods. In fact, she has pictures of him all over her bedroom walls. Like Tiger, Wie hopes to go to Stanford University. She wants to study and play golf.

Wie has other goals, too. She wants to be a regular player on the PGA Tour. And she wants to play the Masters.

The Masters Tournament is one of the most important competitions in golf. It is played at Augusta National in Augusta, Georgia. The course is one of the most beautiful, and one of the most difficult, in golf. It has been won several times by her idol, Tiger Woods. "If I keep working, I think I can get that high," says Wie.

MICHELLE WIE'S HOME AND FAMILY: Michelle lives with her mom and dad in Hawaii. "I play and travel a lot," she says. "But I care about the same things as most kids my age." She likes to read and draw, and her favorite TV show is "Smallville." Boys are not in the picture now. "I don't like boys," she says. "They're kind of annoying."

QUOTE

"I'm not looking to prove a point. I just want to play the best there is."

SOME OF MICHELLE WIE'S RECORDS:

Hawaii State Women's Stroke Play Championship: 2001

Jennie K. Wilson Invitational Championship: 2001

U.S. Women's Amateur Public Links Tournament
  Championship: 2003

FOR MORE INFORMATION ON MICHELLE WIE:

Write: LPGA
        100 International Golf Drive
        Daytona Beach, FL 32124

WORLD WIDE WEB SITE:

http://golf.about.com/cs/womensgolf/a/michellewie.htm

Nancy Willard

1936-
American Author and Poet for
Children and Adults
Creator of *A Visit to William Blake's Inn*

NANCY WILLARD WAS BORN on June 26, 1936, in Ann Arbor, Michigan. Her parents were Hobart and Margaret Willard. Her father was a chemistry professor at the University of Michigan. Her mother was a homemaker. Nancy has one sister.

NANCY WILLARD GREW UP in Ann Arbor. She loved to write and draw from the time she was little. Her parents always encouraged her. Together, they inspired a love of science and art. Her dad was a chemist, so he encouraged her scientific side. Her mother nurtured the artist in her.

"I grew up aware of two ways of looking at the world," recalls Willard. They seem "opposed to each other, and yet can exist side by side in the same person. One is the scientific view. The other is the magic view."

The family spent summers at a nearby lake. With her mom and sister, Nancy loved to explore the natural world. Often, they would take a boat out on the lake. As the boat drifted on the water, her mother would read to them.

Nancy loved to read to herself, too, especially fairy tales, *Alice in Wonderland*, and *The Wizard of Oz*. And she loved to write. When she was just seven, she published her first poem. She wrote and illustrated stories and made little books. She and her sister started a newspaper during their summer vacations at the lake.

CHILDHOOD MEMORIES: Willard has many wonderful memories of her early years. She grew up surrounded with family, including a grandmother and grandfather. She loved to listen to her grandfather recite poetry, loudly, from his room on the third floor.

The ever-curious Nancy liked to find out what the neighbors were up to, too. Her house had a "party line." That was a telephone system in which several families shared the same phone line. You could eavesdrop on your neighbor's conversations. And even though her mother told her never to do that, she did anyway.

Her mother allowed Nancy to cover up the cracks in the walls of their older house with her own paintings. "Whenever a new crack appeared, I fetched my box of paints," she recalled. "My mother and I discussed the possibilities." She painted angels over the cracks in the bathroom, the guest room, and the halls.

She wrote all the time, whenever the spirit moved her. "Reading, drawing, doing my homework, I listened and noted in the margins of my books and math papers and class schedules whatever seemed worth saving: a fragment of speech, a line of poetry."

NANCY WILLARD WENT TO SCHOOL at the local schools in Ann Arbor. She was always a good student, and she won praise and encouragement for her writing. She wrote all kinds of things: essays, poetry, and stories. As a senior in high school, Willard published a poem in the *Horn Book* magazine. That's a fine magazine about children's literature.

Willard stayed in Ann Arbor for college. She attended the University of Michigan and did very well. She majored

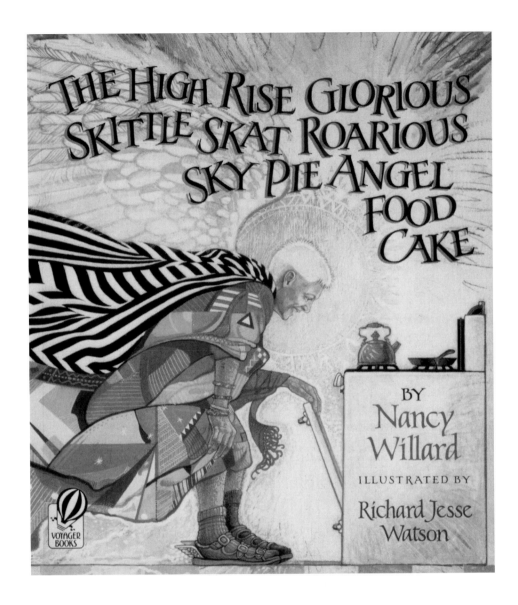

in English, and won several writing awards. Willard graduated from college in 1958.

She wanted to continue studying English, so she went to Stanford University in California. She received her master's degree from Stanford in 1960. Still wanting to study and learn, she went back to Michigan and studied for a PhD. She received that degree in 1963.

FIRST JOBS: Willard's first job after college was at Vassar College in Poughkeepsie, New York. She taught creative writing there. She also continued to write. Her first book was a collection of poetry for adults called *In His Country*. In 1964, she married Eric Lindbloom. Soon they had a son, James Anatole. It was James who inspired Willard to write for kids.

STARTING TO WRITE FOR CHILDREN: In 1974, when James was little, Willard wrote her first children's book. It's called *Sailing to Cythera and Other Anatole Stories*. The character Anatole is a lively little boy who is based on James. The stories feature his adventures in a land full of magic, with talking animals and wizards. Anatole returns in *The Island of the Grass King*, *Stranger's Bread,* and *Uncle Terrible*.

The Anatole books were illustrated by David McPhail. Willard was delighted with the illustrations. "Curiously enough, the drawings do look like James, which pleases and rather astonishes him," she wrote.

James inspired another series, too. In *The Snow Rabbit*, the character named James makes a beautiful bunny out of snow. James returns in *The Well-Mannered*

Balloon. In that book, he paints a pirate face on a balloon, which comes to life at night.

A VISIT TO WILLIAM BLAKE'S INN: POEMS FOR INNO-CENT AND EXPERIENCED TRAVELERS: One of Willard's most beloved books is *A Visit to William Blake's Inn: Poems for Innocent and Experienced Travelers.* It is written as a collection of poems.

The book features William Blake, a famous poet and artist who lived 200 years ago. In Willard's story, Blake owns a magical inn. The poems tell about Blake's life, but also create a fantastic world, where dragons bake bread and angels make beds.

The book is written from the point of view of a seven-year-old girl. In fact, it was inspired by Willard's memories of reading Blake as a child. When she was seven, she got the measles. Her babysitter read her Blake's poem "The Tyger." When she got better, the sitter sent her a collection of Blake's poems. She signed it as if it came from the poet himself. It read: "Poetry is the best medicine."

Before she wrote the book, Willard made a six-foot-tall model of the inn. She made characters and put them in the rooms. She put mirrors on the walls. "Making things with my hands sets the daydreaming process in motion and I begin to *find* the story," she says. "I listen to what's

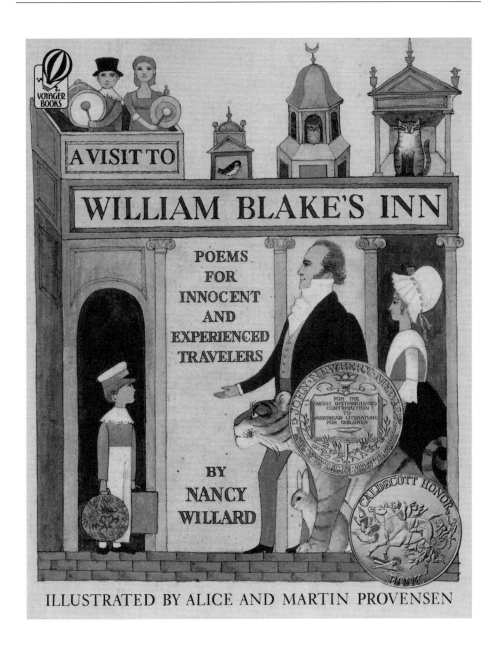

there. I don't make up a story and then make a creature to fit it. It works quite the other way."

A Visit to William Blake's Inn won Willard the Newbery Medal. That is the highest award in children's

books. Willard was delighted with the award, for herself and her illustrators, Alice and Martin Provensen.

THE VOYAGE OF THE LUDGATE HILL: TRAVELS WITH ROBERT LOUIS STEVENSON: Willard features another famous writer in _The Voyage of the Ludgate Hill_. This time the author is Robert Louis Stevenson, the Scottish writer of *Treasure Island* and *Dr. Jekyll and Mr. Hyde*. Willard's book retells the story of Stevenson's travels on a boat carrying fantastic creatures.

Pish, Posh, Said Hieronymous Bosch stars another famous artist from the past. In this book, Willard tells a story about the painter Hieronymous Bosch. Like Bosch's art, the book is full of fantasy.

THE HIGH RISE GLORIOUS SKITTLE SKAT ROARIOUS SKY PIE ANGEL FOOD CAKE: Another favorite book by Willard is *The High Rise Glorious Skittle Skat Roarious Sky Pie Angel Food Cake*. It tells the story of a girl who tries out her great-grandmother's cake recipe. The results are hilarious.

RETELLINGS: Willard has also written books that retell famous fairy tales. In *Cinderella's Dress*, two magpies make Cinderella their adopted daughter. They make Cinderella a glorious dress for the ball. But her wicked stepsisters ruin her gown, and the magpies must find her fairy godmother and resolve the crisis. All ends happily, just in time for the ball.

WORKING WITH ILLUSTRATORS: Willard's books feature art by some of the finest illustrators in children's literature. Artists like Jerry Pinkney, Tomie de Paola, and Emily Arnold McCully have provided beautiful illustrations for her books.

Willard has tried her hand at illustrating, too. In *An Alphabet of Angels* and *The Good-Night Blessing Book* Willard blends photographs and other personal treasures, like postcards, to illustrate her work.

NANCY WILLARD'S HOME AND FAMILY: Willard married Eric Lindbloom in 1964. Eric is a photographer. They have one son, James Anatole. He was featured in several of Willard's books.

Willard lives with her family in upstate New York. She still teaches at Vassar College in Poughkeepsie. She also continues to create all kinds of art, from painting to photography to sculpture.

She has made life-size soft sculptures. Sometimes she takes them with her when she visits schools. Once, she took a creature that later appeared in her book *The Marzipan Moon*. It was strange looking, with ears and antlers, and a middle made out of an old bag of sugar.

Willard set it next to her as she spoke to a class. "If this creature came into school one morning and sat down beside you, what would you do?" she asked. Some of the kids said they would be scared. Some said they would try to be friends with it. She told them that he was from a story she was writing. "In the story 'he' is very real, as real as you are in your life. When you stop to think about it, why can't 'he' be just as real in his world as you are in yours?"

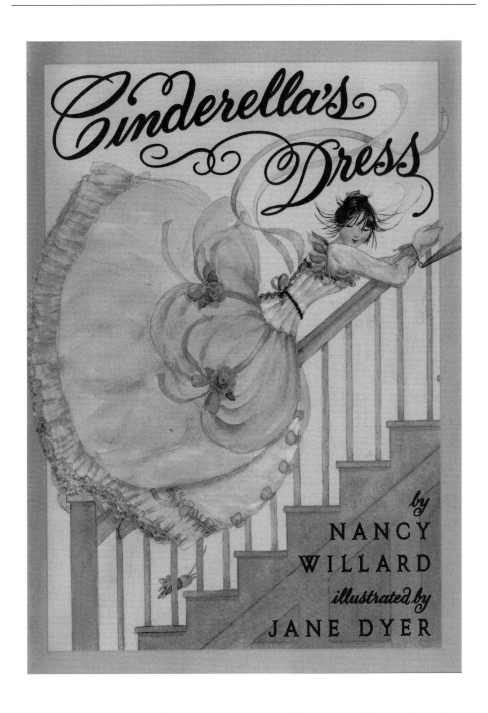

It is that kind of imagination and sense of wonder that makes Willard's books so loved by young readers. And she encourages her readers to create worlds of their own.

QUOTE

"I hope children will want to make their own characters and ask the questions that lead to stories. What if this character came alive? What would it say? What would it eat? Where does it live? What is its name?"

SOME OF NANCY WILLARD'S BOOKS:

Sailing to Cythera and Other Anatole Stories

The Snow Rabbit

The Merry History of a Christmas Pie: With a Delicious Description of a Christmas Soup

The Well-Mannered Balloon

Simple Pictures Are Best

Stranger's Bread

The Highest Hit

The Island of the Grass King: The Further Adventures of Anatole

Papa's Panda

The Marzipan Moon

Uncle Terrible: More Adventures of Anatole

A Visit to William Blake's Inn: Poems for Innocent and Experienced Travelers

The Voyage of the Ludgate Hill: A Journey with Robert Louis Stevenson

The Ballad of Biddy Early

Pish, Posh, Said Hieronymous Bosch

The Nightgown of the Sullen Moon

The Mountains of Quilt

*The High Rise Glorious Skittle Skat Roarious Sky Pie Angel
  Food Cake*

Beauty and the Beast

Cracked Cattle Corn and Snow Ice Cream

An Alphabet of Angels

Among Angels

Gutenberg's Gift

The Good-Night Blessing Book

The Tortilla Cat

The Magic Cornfield

Shadow Story

The Moon and Riddles Diner and the Sunnyside Café

Cinderella's Dress

FOR MORE INFORMATION ABOUT NANCY WILLARD:

Write: Nancy Willard
        Vassar College
        Box 392
        Poughkeepsie, NY 12604-0744

WORLD WIDE WEB SITE:

http://www.writerscenter.org/blumenthalwillard.html

Photo and Illustrations Credits

Ronde and Tiki Barber/Photos: AP/Wide World Photos; Al Bello/Getty Images.

Ludwig Bemelmans/Photo: Walter Sanders/Time Life Pictures/Getty Images. Covers: MADE-LINE (Viking/ PenguinPutnam Books for Young Readers) copyright © Ludwig Bemelmans, 1939. Copyright © renewed Madeline Bemelmans and Barbara Bemelmans Marciano, 1967; MADELINE'S RESCUE (Viking/PenguinPutnam Books for Young Readers) copyright © Ludwig Bemelmans, 1951, 1953. Copyright © renewed Madeline Bemelmans and Barbara Bemelmans Marciano, 1979, 1981; MADELINE AND THE BAD HAT (Puffin Books/Penguin Group) copyright © Ludwig Bemelmans, 1956. Copyright © renewed Madeline Bemelmans and Barbara Bemelmans Marciano, 1984; MADELINE IN LONDON (Puffin Books/ Penguin Group) copyright © Ludwig Bemelmans, 1961. Copyright © renewed Madeline Bemelmans and Barbara Bemelmans Marciano, 1989.

Judy Delton/Photo: Elaine Knox-Wagner. Covers: PEE WEE SCOUTS: TRASH BASH (Dell Publishing/Bantam Doubleday Dell Publishing Group, Inc.) copyright © 1992 by Judy Delton. Illustrations copyright © 1992 by Alan Tiegreen; PEE WEE SCOUTS: BOOKWORM BUDDIES (Dell Publishing/Bantam Doubleday Dell Publishing Group, Inc.) copyright © 1996 by Judy Delton. Illustrations copyright © 1996 by Alan Tiegreen; ANGEL IN CHARGE (Houghton Mifflin) copyright © 1985 by Judy Delton. Illustrations copyright © 1985 by Jill Weber; BACKYARD ANGEL (Houghton Mifflin) copyright © 1983 by Judy Delton. Illustrations copyright © 1999 by Jill Weber.

Raven/Photos: Copyright © Disney; AP/Wide World Photos; Bruce McBroom; Copyright © Disney.

Eric Rohmann/Photo: Courtesy of Millbrook. Covers: TIME FLIES (Dragonfly Books™/ Crown Publishers, Inc.) copyright © 1994 by Eric Rohmann; MY FRIEND RABBIT (Roaring Book Press) copyright © 2002 by Eric Rohmann; PUMPKINHEAD (Borzoi Book/Alfred A. Knopf) copyright © 2003 by Eric Rohmann; THE GOLDEN COMPASS courtesy of Random House Children's Books, a division of Random House, Inc. Cover art copyright © 1996 by Eric Rohmann; THE CINDER-EYED CATS (Crown Publishers, Inc.) copyright © 1997 by Eric Rohmann.

Michelle Wie/Photos: Donald Miralle/Getty Images; AP/Wide World Photos; Jonathan Ferrey/Getty Images.

Nancy Willard/Photo: Eric Lindbloom. Covers: A VISIT TO WILLIAM BLAKE'S INN: POEMS FOR INNOCENT AND EXPERIENCED TRAVELERS (Harcourt Brace Jovanovich Publishers) text copyright © 1981, 1980 by Nancy Willard. Illustrations copyright © 1981 by Alice Provensen and Martin Provensen; THE HIGH RISE GLORIOUS SKITTLE SKAT ROARIOUS SKY PIE ANGEL FOOD CAKE (Voyager Books/Harcourt Brace & Company) text copyright © 1990 by Nancy Willard. Illustrations copyright © 1990 by Richard Jesse Watson; THE VOYAGE OF THE LUDGATE HILL: A JOURNEY WITH ROBERT LOUIS STEVENSON (Harcourt Brace Jovanovich Publishers) text copyright © 1987 by Nancy Willard. Illustrations copyright © 1987 by Alice Provensen and Martin Provensen; CINDERELLA'S DRESS (Blue Sky Press/Scholastic) text copyright © 2003 by Nancy Willard. Illustrations copyright © 2003 by Jane Dyer.

Name Index

Listed below are the names of all individuals who have appeared in *Biography for Beginners,* followed by the issue and year in which they appear.

Aguilera, Christina,
  Spring 2001
Aliki, Spring '96
Allen, Tim, Fall '96
Annan, Kofi, Fall 2000
Applegate, K.A., Spring 2000
Armstrong, Lance, Fall 2002
Avi, Spring 2003

Ballard, Robert, Fall 2002
Barber, Ronde, Spring 2004
Barber, Tiki, Spring 2004
Bemelmans, Ludwig,
  Spring 2004
Bentley, Wilson
  "Snowflake", Spring 2003
Berenstain, Jan, Fall '95
Berenstain, Stan, Fall '95
Blair, Bonnie, Spring '95
Blume, Judy, Fall '95
Bonds, Barry, Fall 2002
Brandy, Fall '96
Brett, Jan, Spring '95
Bridwell, Norman, Fall '99
Brown, Marc, Spring '98
Bryan, Zachery Ty,
  Spring '97

Bryant, Kobe, Fall '99
Bunting, Eve, Fall 2001
Burton, LeVar, Spring '98
Burton, Virginia Lee,
  Spring '97
Bush, George W., Fall 2001
Bush, Laura, Spring 2002
Butcher, Susan, Fall 2000
Byars, Betsy, Fall 2002

Cannon, Janell, Spring '99
Cannon, Nick, Spring 2003
Carle, Eric, Spring '95
Carson, Ben, Fall 2003
Carter, Vince, Fall 2001
Cheney, Dick, Fall 2003
Christopher, Matt, Fall '97
Cleary, Beverly, Spring '95
Clinton, Bill, Spring '95
Clinton, Chelsea, Fall '96
Clinton, Hillary, Spring '96
Cole, Joanna, Fall '95
Cooney, Barbara,
  Spring 2001
Crews, Donald, Fall '99
Curtis, Christopher Paul,
  Spring 2000

Dahl, Roald, Fall 2000
Danziger, Paula, Fall 2001
Davis, Jim, Fall '95
Delton, Judy, Spring 2004
dePaola, Tomie, Spring '98
Duff, Hilary, Spring 2003

Earle, Sylvia, Fall '99
Ehlert, Lois, Fall 2000
Ellerbee, Linda, Fall 2003
Estefan, Gloria, Spring '96

Falconer, Ian, Fall 2003

Geisel, Theodor Seuss
 see **Seuss, Dr.**, Spring '95
Giff, Patricia Reilly,
 Spring 2001
Ginsburg, Ruth Bader,
 Fall 2000
Goodall, Jane, Spring '96
Gordon, Jeff, Spring 2000
Gore, Al, Fall '97
GrandPré, Mary, Fall 2003
Gretzky, Wayne, Spring '96
Griffey, Ken Jr., Fall '95

Hamilton, Virginia, Fall '99
Hamm, Mia, Spring '98
Hart, Melissa Joan, Fall '95
Hawk, Tony, Fall 2001

Henkes, Kevin, Fall '98
Henson, Jim, Fall '96
Hill, Grant, Fall '97
Horner, Jack, Spring '97
Houston, Whitney,
 Spring '98

Irwin, Steve, Spring 2003

Jemison, Mae, Fall '96
Jeter, Derek, Fall 2000
Johnson, Lonnie,
 Spring 2002
Jones, Marion, Spring 2001
Jordan, Michael, Spring '97
Joyner-Kersee, Jackie,
 Fall '95

Keats, Ezra Jack, Fall '95
Kellogg, Steven,
 Spring 2001
Kerrigan, Nancy, Fall '95
Kwan, Michelle,
 Spring 2002

Lasseter, John, Fall 2002
Lewis, Shari, Spring '99
Lin, Maya, Spring 2001
Lindgren, Astrid, Fall 2002
Lionni, Leo, Spring '99
Lipinski, Tara, Spring '98

Subject Index

This index includes subjects, occupations, and ethnic and minority origins for individuals who have appeared in *Biography for Beginners.*

Australian
Irwin, Steve, Spring 2003

authors
Aliki, Spring '96
Applegate, K.A.,
   Spring 2000
Avi, Spring 2003
Bemelmans, Ludwig,
   Spring 2004
Berenstain, Jan, Fall '95
Berenstain, Stan, Fall, '95
Blume, Judy, Fall '95
Brett, Jan, Spring '95
Bridwell, Norman, Fall '99
Brown, Marc, Spring '98
Bunting, Eve, Fall 2001
Burton, Virginia Lee,
   Spring '97
Byars, Betsy, Fall 2002
Cannon, Janell, Spring '99
Carle, Eric, Spring '95
Carson, Ben, Fall 2003
Christopher, Matt, Fall '97
Cleary, Beverly, Spring '95
Cole, Joanna, Fall '95
Cooney, Barbara,
   Spring 2001
Crews, Donald, Fall '99
Curtis, Christopher Paul,
   Spring 2000
Dahl, Roald, Fall 2000

Danziger, Paula, Fall 2001
Delton, Judy, Spring 2004
dePaola, Tomie, Spring '98
Ehlert, Lois, Fall 2000
Ellerbee, Linda, Fall 2003
Falconer, Ian, Fall 2003
Giff, Patricia Reilly,
   Spring 2001
Hamilton, Virginia, Fall '99
Henkes, Kevin, Fall '98
Keats, Ezra Jack, Fall '95
Kellogg, Steven, Spring 2001
Lindgren, Astrid, Fall 2002
Lionni, Leo, Spring '99
Lobel, Arnold, Spring '95
MacLachlan, Patricia,
   Spring 2003
Marshall, James, Fall '97
Martin, Ann M., Spring '96
Mayer, Mercer, Spring '97
McCloskey, Robert,
   Fall 2003
McKissack, Fredrick,
   Fall '98
McKissack, Patricia,
   Fall '98
Myers, Walter Dean,
   Fall 2001
Numeroff, Laura, Fall '99
Osborne, Mary Pope,
   Fall 2001
Parish, Peggy, Spring '97

GrandPré, Mary, Fall 2003

Hamilton, Virginia, Fall '99

Hamm, Mia, Spring '98

Hart, Melissa Joan, Fall '95

Houston, Whitney,
  Spring '98

Jemison, Mae, Fall '96

Jones, Marion, Spring 2001

Joyner-Kersee, Jackie,
  Fall '95

Kerrigan, Nancy, Fall '95

Kwan, Michelle,
  Spring 2002

Lewis, Shari, Spring '99

Lin, Maya, Spring 2001

Lindgren, Astrid, Fall 2002

Lipinski, Tara, Spring '98

Lucid, Shannon, Fall '97

MacLachlan, Patricia,
  Spring 2003

Martin, Ann M., Spring '96

McKissack, Patricia, Fall '98

Miller, Shannon, Spring '95

Moceanu, Dominique,
  Fall '98

Nechita, Alexandra,
  Spring 2000

Numeroff, Laura, Fall '99

O'Donnell, Rosie, Fall '99

Oleynik, Larisa, Spring '96

Olsen, Ashley, Spring '95

Olsen, Mary-Kate, Spring '95

Osborne, Mary Pope,
  Fall 2001

Parish, Peggy, Spring '97

Park, Barbara, Spring '98

Parks, Rosa, Fall '95

Polacco, Patricia, Fall '97

Potter, Beatrix, Fall '98

Raven, Spring 2004

Rice, Condoleezza,
  Spring 2002

Ringgold, Faith, Spring '99

Rowling, J.K., Fall 2000

Rylant, Cynthia, Fall '96

Scurry, Briana, Fall '99

Strug, Kerri, Spring '97

Swoopes, Sheryl,
  Spring 2000

Teresa, Mother, Fall '98

Van Dyken, Amy,
  Spring 2000

Wells, Rosemary, Spring '96

Wie, Michelle, Spring 2004

Wilder, Laura Ingalls,
  Fall '96

Willard, Nancy, Spring 2004

Williams, Serena, Fall 2003

Wilson, Mara, Spring '97

Winfrey, Oprah, Fall 2002

Wood, Audrey, Spring 2003

Yamaguchi, Kristi, Fall '97

Yolen, Jane, Spring '99

scientists
Ballard, Robert, Fall 2002
Carson, Ben, Fall 2003
Earle, Sylvia, Fall '99
Goodall, Jane, Spring '96
Horner, Jack, Spring '97
Jemison, Mae, Fall '96
Johnson, Lonnie,
    Spring 2002
Lucid, Shannon, Fall '97
Satcher, David,
    Spring 2000

Secretary General of the United Nations
Annan, Kofi, Fall 2000

set designer
Falconer, Ian, Fall 2003

skateboarder
Hawk, Tony, Fall 2001

skaters
Blair, Bonnie, Spring '95
Kerrigan, Nancy, Fall '95
Kwan, Michelle,
    Spring 2002
Lipinski, Tara, Spring '98
Yamaguchi, Kristi, Fall '97

sled-dog racing
Butcher, Susan, Fall 2000

soccer players
Hamm, Mia, Spring '98
Pele, Spring '97
Scurry, Briana, Fall '99

South African
Mandela, Nelson, Spring '95

Supreme Court Justice
Ginsburg, Ruth Bader,
    Fall 2000

Surgeon General of the U.S.
Satcher, David, Spring 2000

Swedish
Lindgren, Astrid, Fall 2002

swimmer
Van Dyken, Amy,
    Spring 2000

television
Allen, Tim, Fall '96
Brandy, Fall '96
Bryan, Zachery Ty,
    Spring '97
Burton, LeVar, Spring '98
Cannon, Nick, Spring 2003
Duff, Hilary, Spring 2003
Ellerbee, Linda, Fall 2003
Hart, Melissa Joan, Fall '95

Irwin, Steve, Spring 2003
Lewis, Shari, Spring '99
Muniz, Frankie, Fall 2001
Nye, Bill, Spring '99
O'Donnell, Rosie, Fall '99
Oleynik, Larisa, Spring '96
Olsen, Ashley, Spring '95
Olsen, Mary-Kate,
  Spring '95
Raven, Spring 2004
Rogers, Fred, Fall '98
Thomas, Jonathan Taylor,
  Fall '95
White, Jaleel, Fall '97
Winfrey, Oprah, Fall 2002

tennis
Williams, Serena, Fall 2003

United Nations
Annan, Kofi, Fall 2000

**Vice President of the
United States**
Cheney, Dick, Fall 2003
Gore, Al, Fall '97

Birthday Index

January
12 John Lasseter (1957)
14 Shannon Lucid (1943)
17 Shari Lewis (1934)
21 Hakeem Olajuwon (1963)
26 Vince Carter (1977)
28 Wayne Gretzky (1961)
29 Bill Peet (1915)
   Rosemary Wells (1943)
   Oprah Winfrey (1954)
30 Dick Cheney (1941)

February
4 Rosa Parks (1913)
7 Laura Ingalls Wilder (1867)
9 Wilson "Snowflake" Bentley (1865)
11 Jane Yolen (1939)
   Brandy (1979)
12 Judy Blume (1938)
   David Small (1945)
13 Mary GrandPré (1954)
15 Norman Bridwell (1928)
   Amy Van Dyken (1973)
16 LeVar Burton (1957)
17 Michael Jordan (1963)
22 Steve Irwin (1962)
27 Chelsea Clinton (1980)

March
2 Dr. Seuss (1904)
   David Satcher (1941)
3 Patricia MacLachlan (1938)
   Jackie Joyner-Kersee (1962)
4 Garrett Morgan (1877)
   Dav Pilkey (1966)
5 Jake Lloyd (1989)
10 Shannon Miller (1977)
11 Ezra Jack Keats (1916)
12 Virginia Hamilton (1936)
15 Ruth Bader Ginsburg (1933)
16 Shaquille O'Neal (1972)
17 Mia Hamm (1972)
18 Bonnie Blair (1964)
20 Fred Rogers (1928)
   Louis Sachar (1954)
21 Rosie O'Donnell (1962)
25 Sheryl Swoopes (1971)
31 Al Gore (1948)

April
3 Jane Goodall (1934)
5 Colin Powell (1937)
7 RondeBarber (1975)
   Tiki Barber (1975)

April (continued)
 8 Kofi Annan (1938)
12 Beverly Cleary (1916)
   Tony Hawk (1968)
16 Garth Williams (1912)
18 Melissa Joan Hart
   (1976)
26 Patricia Reilly Giff
   (1935)
27 Ludwig Bemelmans
   (1898)
   Barbara Park (1947)

May
 4 Don Wood (1945)
 6 Judy Delton (1931)
10 Leo Lionni (1910)
   Christopher Paul
   Curtis (1953)
14 Emmitt Smith (1969)
17 Gary Paulsen (1939)
20 Mary Pope Osborne
   (1949)
22 Arnold Lobel (1933)

June
 5 Richard Scarry (1919)
 6 Cynthia Rylant (1954)
 7 Larisa Oleynik (1981)
10 Maurice Sendak (1928)
   Tara Lipinski (1982)
11 Joe Montana (1956)

13 Tim Allen (1953)
15 Jack Horner (1946)
18 Chris Van Allsburg
   (1949)
25 Eric Carle (1929)
26 Nancy Willard (1936)
   Derek Jeter (1974)
   Michael Vick (1980)
30 Robert Ballard (1971)

July
 2 Dave Thomas (1932)
 6 George W. Bush (1946)
 7 Michelle Kwan (1980)
11 E.B. White (1899)
   Patricia Polacco (1944)
12 Kristi Yamaguchi
   (1972)
14 Peggy Parish (1927)
   Laura Numeroff (1953)
18 Nelson Mandela (1918)
24 Barry Bonds (1964)
   Mara Wilson (1987)
26 Jan Berenstain (1923)
28 Beatrix Potter (1866)
   Jim Davis (1945)
31 J.K. Rowling (1965)
   Daniel Radcliffe (1989)

August
 2 Betsy Byars (1928)
 4 Jeff Gordon (1971)

August (continued)

- **6** Barbara Cooney (1917)
  David Robinson (1965)
- **9** Patricia McKissack (1944)
  Whitney Houston (1963)
- **11** Joanna Cole (1944)
- **12** Walter Dean Myers (1937)
  Fredrick McKissack (1939)
  Ann M. Martin (1955)
- **15** Linda Ellerbee (1944)
- **16** Matt Christopher (1917)
- **18** Paula Danziger (1944)
- **19** Bill Clinton (1946)
- **23** Kobe Bryant (1978)
- **24** Cal Ripken Jr. (1960)
- **26** Mother Teresa (1910)
- **27** Alexandra Nechita (1985)
- **30** Virginia Lee Burton (1909)
  Sylvia Earle (1935)
  Donald Crews (1938)
- **31** Itzhak Perlman (1945)

September

- **1** Gloria Estefan (1958)
- **3** Aliki (1929)
- **7** Briana Scurry (1971)
- **8** Jack Prelutsky (1940)
  Jon Scieszka (1954)
  Jonathan Taylor Thomas (1982)
- **15** McCloskey, Robert (1914)
  Tomie dePaola (1934)
- **16** Roald Dahl (1916)
- **18** Ben Carson (1951)
  Lance Armstrong (1971)
- **24** Jim Henson (1936)
- **25** Will Smith (1968)
- **26** Serena Williams (1981)
- **28** Hilary Duff (1987)
- **29** Stan Berenstain (1923)
- **30** Dominique Moceanu (1981)

October

- **1** Mark McGwire (1963)
- **5** Grant Hill (1972)
  Maya Lin (1959)
- **6** Lonnie Johnson (1949)
- **7** Yo-Yo Ma (1955)
- **8** Faith Ringgold (1930)
- **9** Zachery Ty Bryan (1981)
- **10** James Marshall (1942)
- **11** Michelle Wie (1989)
- **12** Marion Jones (1975)
- **13** Nancy Kerrigan (1969)

October (continued)
17 Mae Jemison (1954)
Nick Cannon (1980)
18 Wynton Marsalis (1961)
22 Ichiro Suzuki (1973)
23 Pele (1940)
25 Pedro Martinez (1971)
26 Hillary Clinton (1947)
Steven Kellogg (1941)
Eric Rohmann (1957)

November
3 Janell Cannon (1957)
4 Laura Bush (1946)
9 Lois Ehlert (1934)
12 Sammy Sosa (1968)
14 Astrid Lindgren (1907)
William Steig (1907)
Condoleezza Rice
(1954)
15 Daniel Pinkwater
(1941)
19 Kerri Strug (1977)
21 Ken Griffey Jr. (1969)
25 Marc Brown (1946)
26 Charles Schulz (1922)
27 Bill Nye (1955)
Kevin Henkes (1960)
Jaleel White (1977)

December
1 Jan Brett (1949)
5 Frankie Muniz (1985)
10 Raven (1985)
18 Christina Aguilera
(1980)
19 Eve Bunting (1928)
22 Jerry Pinkney (1939)
23 Avi (1937)
26 Susan Butcher (1954)
30 Mercer Mayer (1943)
Tiger Woods (1975)